T0194216

In Case You're Still Here

By Demond M James

authorHOUSE®

AuthorHouse™
1663 Liberty Drive
Bloomington, IN 47403
www.authorhouse.com
Phone: 1-800-839-8640

First published by AuthorHouse 5/4/2011

ISBN: 978-1-4567-6832-4 (e)
ISBN: 978-1-4567-6831-7 (sc)

Library of Congress Control Number: 2011907106

Printed in the United States of America

Any people depicted in stock imagery provided by Thinkstock are models, and such images are being used for illustrative purposes only. Certain stock imagery © Thinkstock.

All Scripture quotations are taken from the King James Version of the Holy Bible unless otherwise noted.

This book is printed on acid-free paper.

For God has not given us the spirit of fear but that of power, and of love, and of a sound mind. 2 Timothy 1:7

Introduction

Eschatology is the study of end-time events as outlined in Scripture. If you are reading this book, then either you have a strong interest in eschatology, you are entertained by it, or something has transpired.

My guess is either the first option or the last. If it is the first, then you have chosen the right book to start learning more about God's plan for humanity and this world. This book is simple in understanding basic end-time events in an easy-to-understand outline. If it is the latter, then this is the right book to help you to know and understand more about what is happening to you and the rest of the world.

I pray that all is well and that everyone may hear what the Spirit saith. May God continue to bless you and be with you throughout your journey.

Dedication

This book is dedicated to those who are close to me but have yet to accept and truly believe the Lord Jesus Christ and His will for their lives: Nathaniel, Kevin, Latasha, Ralph, Corri, Lorenzo, Leonardo—and to those who are closely related and connected to these individuals. To the unbeliever. To the elect and those who are familiar with the Word but with whom the Word is not familiar. Please share this book with each other and others outside of your inner and outer circles. May you all be blessed. Let him who hath an ear hear what the Spirit says (the body once called the church has been lifted up).

For my daughters Destiney, Ajia, and Cynaiah.

Table of Contents

Chapter One
Where Are They Now?

There is coming a time when peace will suddenly be taken from the earth. You ask why would peace be taken from the earth? Revelation 6:4 says, "There went out another horse that was red: and power was given to him that sat thereon to take peace from the earth." This is the second of seven seal judgments that are being released at the end of the age commonly called the church age or the age of the dispensation of grace. From the beginning of civilization up until this future time, there have been wars and conflict all over the world, but never has peace been taken from the entire world at one time. *Peace* is a condition of the mind based on private and public order, or the absence of confusion. It is concord, harmony, or an undisturbed state of mind. So could it be that this man who comes on this horse is given power to take peace from the Earth not by initiating open war, but by his initial appearance? Second Thessalonians 2:3 says, "Let no man deceive you by any means: for that day shall not come, except there come a falling away first, and that man of sin be revealed, the son of perdition." The previous verse encourages its readers not to be shaken or troubled in their mind because the day of the Lord has not yet begun. In other words they should retain their peace before this man makes his world debut. What happens after he is introduced to the world that interrupts peace? What triggers that day coming is the revealing of the man of sin. So what exactly takes peace from the Earth?

Imagine for one second that you're with someone, maybe a friend or relative, spouse or coworker, and before you can barely blink your eyes, something happens and you look up and they are gone without a trace, without a clue. You look and feel all around, but the other person is not there. You yell out for him or her, but still there is no answer. He or she just disappeared or vanished into thin air. The only thing remaining from that person is maybe the clothing that he or she was wearing while with you. Things happened so fast that you didn't see what happened to the other person. They were so quick that even the cameras and video surveillance didn't capture what happened. Things changed in a flash, in the twinkling of an eye, and at the speed of lightning. "Then shall two be in the field; the one shall be taken and the other left. Two women shall be grinding at the mill; the one shall be taken and the other left" (Matthew 24:40–41). Now in enters chaos.

As if things were not already bad enough. Take a look around and you see worldwide famine in places where there once was abundance. The price of food has doubled and in some cases tripled from just a short time ago. Gas prices are soaring almost astronomically, it seems. Tensions are escalating in the Middle East. You see wars and fighting except where there is a peace agreement. There are things occurring in the world that have never happened before, such as earthquakes occurring in different places than usual. Within the past 1–50 years we have seen new diseases come from virtually nowhere: West Nile virus; monkey virus; mad cow disease; HIV/AIDS; dengue fever; hand, foot, and mouth disease; SARS; bird flu; etc. The stars and the heavens are also affected. There are signs in the stars that tell of a change of the times and in the atmosphere. NASA continues to make discoveries about the solar system. There are clusters of stars, gases, and dust that have the appearance of human body parts, and NASA has named two of them the Eye of God and the Hand of God. Then there is what looks like a crown of thorns and the group of stars, gases, and dust particles that looks like a cross.

Now return to our previous scenario. With all of these things happening all over the world, at this time your companion suddenly disappears. Cars begin to crash and get into accidents; the expressways are jammed. Airplanes are diving and being diverted. The workforce is collapsing because the key components have vanished. Stock markets worldwide are crashing. Banks and investment companies are folding. Crimes are becoming more vicious and malicious and have become more frequent. Evil activity has increased in the earth and has possessed more people, causing them to commit heinous crimes. You think to yourself, *how could my loved ones possibly leave me at a time like this? How could they just take off and leave? Did they not love me? Did they not care? Why didn't they take me with them? And where are they now?* We'll seek answers to these and other questions, and we will find answers by examining the Word of God and what it has to say about these things and other relative issues.

Earlier, I mentioned a scene that is described in Matthew 24:40–41 where two people are seen together, then there is only one. Some scholars believe that this scene shows the second coming of Christ. If this is the second coming of Christ, then that means that Christ here is returning to earth to rule and reign. So if he is coming to reign, then why is only one taken (present tense), and who is doing the taking, and where is the person being taken to? Assuming that this viewpoint is correct, then those who are left would have to be allowed to rule and reign with Christ. And those who are taken would have to enter into some type of judgment or hell, or be destroyed. Scripture does not specifically say that they were killed or sent to hell or judged. It says that they were taken.

First, let's look at Matthew 24. This chapter is what is called the Olivet Discourse. This discourse or sermon was given by Jesus on the Mount of Olives. His audience was four of his disciples: Peter, James, John, and Andrew. The discourse can be viewed as an acronym—(O)ut (LI)ne of (V)(E)nd (T)imes—for outline of end times. It can also be found in Luke 21:5–38, and Mark 13 in its entirety. The disciples, after hearing Jesus speak of the imminent destruction of the temple, questioned Jesus about the timing of the things that he spoke about, the sign of his coming (back), and the sign of the end of the age (not "world" as was mistranslated). Jesus gave them and us answers and clues to the things that they were inquiring about in what is called the Olivet Discourse. The Olivet Discourse covers different events surrounding the return of our Lord Jesus Christ. These events are somewhat but not necessarily in any chronological order. The reason that I believe the scene in Matthew 24:40–41 is referring to Jesus' rapture of the church is because in verse 42 it says, "Watch therefore: for ye know not what hour your Lord doth come." The next verse talks of a parable of a breaking and entering of a house with the thief going unnoticed. It was something that occurred unexpectedly and quickly. After the rapture of the church the timing of the Lord can be determined by Scripture. The timing of the Lord's return after the Rapture is approximately seven years (Daniel 9:27). If this passage was speaking of the Second Coming, it would not be a sudden unexpected event at this point.

Now the second coming of Jesus is the fourth major event concerning his return. The parable of the fig tree gives us a clue on when the seven major events will start to occur. The fig tree is symbolic of Israel. Since the destruction of the temple in AD 70, Israel had not existed as a nation until they were reestablished as such in 1948. For approximately 1,900 years they did not exist; then, just as Scripture predicted, they once again became a nation. Matthew 24:32 says, "Now learn a parable of the fig tree; when his branch is yet tender, and putteth forth leaves, ye know that summer is nigh: So likewise ye, when you shall see all these things, know that it is near, even at the doors. Verily, I say unto you, this generation shall not pass, til all these things be fulfilled." Well, we have to determine what a generation is.

Some would say that a generation is about forty years. Forty is the number of years that the nation of Israel spent in the wilderness. Also, it is the number of days that Jesus spent in the wilderness and was tempted of the devil. It is the number of days that Moses spent up in the mountain, and it is the number of days that he and Elijah fasted. Thirty-nine is the number of chastisement (2 Corinthians 11:24). Forty is the number of testing, not the number of a generation. In the flood of Noah's day, it rained forty days and forty nights. Moses spent forty days on Mount Sinai. The Israelite spies surveyed the Promised Land for forty days and were then asked if they could possess the land. Elijah ran two hundred miles in forty days. Israel was challenged by Goliath for forty days while God prepared David to face the biblical giant. God sent Jonah to Nineveh with a message of impending destruction unless they changed their ways of idolatry and worshipping false gods, and they changed in forty days. The disciples spent forty days with Jesus after his resurrection.

Nowhere in the Bible does the number forty refer to a generation or the span of a person's life. Testing is the main theme biblically of the number forty. A generation in Bible times and today is approximately seventy years. Psalms 90:10 says, "The days of our years are threescore years and ten," which is the number seventy. Of course people lived longer than this in every generation from creation until today. But today the average life span of a person is approximately seventy years of age. The time span from the reestablishment of Israel as a nation in 1948 up until now nearly fulfills a generation. The time is near. Summer is now officially here! In order to get more answers to our questions, let's take an even closer look into the Word of God to get answers and clues to the question, where are they now? And more!

Chapter Two
Caught Up

"And Enoch walked with God after he begat Methuselah three hundred years, and begat sons and daughters: And all the days of Enoch were three hundred sixty and five years: And Enoch walked with God: and he was not: for God took him" (Genesis 5:22–24). Enoch, whose name means "initiated or dedicated," was the first person mentioned in Scripture that "skipped" death. The Bible says that he "was not." How can someone be or exist one second and the very next become "not," or nonexistent? Hebrews 11:5 says, "By faith Enoch was translated [taken] that he should not see death; and was not found, because God had translated him: for before his translation he had this testimony, that he pleased God." The verse implies that Enoch could not be located. He was touchable, visible, and identifiable one minute and then the next he was gone. When defining the word *translate*, we get this definition: "to move from one place or condition to another; to transfer; to convey directly to heaven without death."

Enoch was taken by God himself directly to heaven without dying. Why would God take Enoch or anyone directly to heaven—especially since from Adam on, every person was sentenced to die? Genesis 2:17 says, "But of the tree of the knowledge of good and evil, thou shalt not eat of it; for in the day that thou eatest thereof thou shalt surely die." When Adam and Eve disobeyed God by eating of the tree, it caused the fall of man, which we call sin, in turn, causing death upon mankind. Every human that is born after Adam inherits a sinful nature, and with that sinful nature comes the consequence of death. But here, Enoch somehow escapes death. We know very little about Enoch except what is mentioned in Genesis 5:18–24; 1 Chronicles 1:3; and Hebrews 11:5, where it talks about Enoch's faith: "By faith Enoch was translated that he should not see death; and was not found, because God had translated him: for before his translation he had this testimony, that he pleased God."

By taking a look back in Genesis we can see how he pleased God. After the fall of man, sin became more prevalent and more acceptable in that time. The first murder is recorded in Genesis 4:8 of Abel by his brother Cain. Verse 24 of the same chapter shows the progression and passiveness of sin and how quickly it had adapted and become more acceptable. Lamech killed a young man for wounding him or trying to kill him, and he boasted about the killing to his two wives. Not only that, but he also said that if anyone tried to avenge the murder, that he would take care of himself without any help from God, the way that God took care of Cain. So we see that sin had spread like wildfire. And there seemed to be a disregard for God. Ever since sin entered into the world, direct interaction with God, such as when God visited Adam in the cool of the day, had ceased.

The Scriptures say that "Enoch walked with God." That means that he had fellowship with God. He had respect for God and his law despite all the sin and the apostasy that was around him. In a world that disregarded God, Enoch followed His word. He was different from everyone else; in fact, his name means "initiated or dedicated." Before he was born he was to be dedicated to God. Enoch didn't waver in his faith either. The Bible says that he walked with God for three hundred years after he begot Methuselah. He literally carried God's word with him in his heart and his mind. He pleased God to the point where God took Enoch to be with Him.

Enoch was one of only two men mentioned in the Bible who were translated. Translation was the act of being taken to heaven without tasting (seeing) death. The other person mentioned in Scripture who was taken to heaven without tasting death is the prophet Elijah. Second Kings chapter 2:1-11 details the events leading up to the translation of Elijah: "And it came to pass when the Lord would take up Elijah into heaven by a whirlwind that Elijah went with Elisha from Gilgal." First, it is important to note that Elijah was well aware that the Lord would take him. It was not a secret, nor was this revelation hidden to the people in

Elijah's day. Secondly, it is also important to note that the disciples of the school of the prophets also were aware of this revelation. Verse 3 says, "And the sons of the prophets that were at Bethel came forth to Elisha, and said unto him, knowest thou that the Lord will take away thy master from thy head today? And he said, Yea, I know it; hold ye your peace." Thirdly, Elisha knew of this coming, inevitable translation. Notice the response of Elisha, he said, "yea, I know." So Elijah, the prophets, and Elisha knew of this translation. It was no secret that the Lord was going to translate his servant Elijah. This action is referred to by Christians as "being caught up." Today, the term used by Christians to refer to this act is the Rapture.

The act of being caught up was revealed to the apostle Paul. He shared (discussed) this revelation with the people at the church at Thessalonica when they were anxiously awaiting the return of Jesus. The Thessalonians were restless and had stopped working because they believed that Jesus was coming soon to make his return to earth to establish his kingdom and bring them with him. They had concerns about what would happen when Jesus returned for their fellow servants who followed Christ but had passed away. 1Thessalonians 4:14–17 says, "For this we say unto you by the word of the Lord, that we which are alive and remain unto the coming of the Lord shall not prevent them which are asleep. For the Lord himself shall descend from heaven with a shout, with the voice of the archangel, and with the trump of God: and the dead in Christ shall rise first. Then we which are alive and remain shall be caught up together with them in the clouds, to meet the Lord in the air: and so shall we ever be with the Lord."

In the first century the last trump (shofar) meant a specific day of the year. In Judaism there are three trumpets (the shofarim) that have a name. The first trump, the last trump, and the great trump. Each one indicates a specific day in the Jewish calendar. The first trump is blown on the feast of Shavuot (Pentecost). It proclaimed that God had betrothed himself to Israel. The last trump is blown on what is known today as Rosh Hashanah. It is the same day that Leviticus 23:23–24 calls the Feast of Trumpets. It is also referred to as a Sabbath, a rest day or a holy day, a memorial of blowing of trumpets, a holy convocation, and the day of trumpets. The Great trump is blown on what is called Yom Kippur (Day of Atonement), which will herald the return of the Messiah back to earth. This day is symbolically and prophetically synonymous with the Second Coming of Christ.

The Mosaic festival year started in the month of Passover and was seven months long. At the beginning of each month, the trump was sounded. The seventh month, the month of Tishri, was the last month of the Mosaic year. Tishri was the start of or the first month of the Jewish civil year. On the first day of the month of Tishri, the last trump of the Mosaic year was blown. That is what Paul meant in 1 Corinthians 15:52 when he said, "In a moment in the twinkling of an eye, at the last trump: for the trumpet shall sound, and the dead shall be raised incorruptible, and we shall be changed." The day of the last trump was the first day of the month of Tishri. This verse would be well understood by Jews but would not be understood by Gentiles who had no knowledge of the Jewish calendar or the seven feasts of Israel. It is the same thing that Paul meant when he wrote to the church at Thessalonica and said, "For the Lord himself shall descend from heaven with a shout, with the voice of the archangel, and with the trump of God: and the dead in Christ shall rise first."

To understand the significance of this particular day you would have to have some knowledge of the feasts and the customs of the day and of the Jewish people. Early Jews recognized the Day of Trumpets as a memorial day for those who have died. It was not the same type of memorial day that we are used to, but it is a symbolic time when the dead return to be rejoined with their descendants at the beginning of the year. The beginning of the year for Israel is in the month of Tishri, the seventh month of the Mosaic festival year, which is equivalent to our mid-September to mid-October. Other significant events that occurred at the start of the Jewish New Year are the creation of the world, Noah's birthday and the flood of his time, Joseph's release from prison and elevation in the kingdom (also in the year of Jubilee), and the actual birth of Jesus Christ. The Day of Trumpets is related to what is known as the Rapture and will occur precisely at this time. It is outlined in Leviticus 23:23–25 (today known by Israel and the Jews as Rosh Hashanah) and is symbolic of and points to, prophetically, the rapture of the church.

God's church can be described as all those who have professed belief in Jesus Christ, from the time of the Resurrection and Ascension to the time of the second coming of Christ.

The Rapture is a belief that God will come and take his church from

Earth to heaven before His wrath comes to the world to try those who dwell on Earth (Revelation 3:10) at that time during the Tribulation as described in Revelation 6–18. This belief is challenged by some because the word *rapture* is not mentioned anywhere in the Bible. However, the word *Bible* is also not mentioned in the Bible, and neither is *trinity*. The word *millennium* is not found anywhere in the Bible, but the phrase "thousand-year reign" is. The Bible does not use *demon*, but we do find *evil spirit*. That these words are not specifically mentioned doesn't mean that the Bible does not teach them or allude to them or that they do not exist. The Bible is a firm proponent of the Bible, the Trinity, the Millennium, and the Rapture. The concept is clearly there in Scripture though it is not mentioned. In fact, in the Latin Vulgate, the word *rapturo* is mentioned specifically, and that's where we get our English word *rapture*.

This event has been expected by the church since it was revealed through the apostle Paul that this would be the first of two parts in the way in which Christ would make his return to earth. Titus 2:13 says "Looking for that blessed hope and the glorious appearing of the great God and our Saviour Jesus Christ." The first part of the return of Jesus focuses on the rapture of the church. That's what is called the blessed hope of the church. The church earnestly looks for Jesus to come and rescue them from impending danger. As a matter of fact, the term *rapture* means "to snatch up or to seize up out of danger." This would be like picking a little baby up out of the way of danger. Think of a child running into the street while playing, not knowing that a semi truck is speeding in his direction. The parent quickly springs up and rushes toward the child and the approaching semi, and snatches the child out of harm's way. That is exactly what the Rapture is—God snatching his children out of the way of danger. Revelation 3:10 says, "Because thou hast kept the word of my patience, I also will keep thee from the hour of temptation, which shall come upon all the world, to try them that dwell upon the earth."

That is what will happen to the people. They won't be abducted by aliens, they won't be in space, and they won't be somewhere hiding. They will be taken directly to heaven just like Enoch and Elijah were. The only difference between these two men and the church is that these two men have to return as the two witnesses of Revelation 11 to restore all things. When the church is taken up, it will experience at the same time what is called the first resurrection. The first resurrection will be held in two parts. The first will be the resurrection of the dead in Christ and the living in Christ (Rapture). "Behold, I show you a mystery; We shall not all sleep, but we shall all be changed, In a moment, in the twinkling of an eye, at the last trump: for the trumpet shall sound, and the dead shall be raised incorruptible, and we shall be changed" (1 Corinthians 15:51–52). The second part will be the resurrection of the Tribulation saints and the Old Testament saints at the end of the Tribulation period. "And at that time shall Michael stand up, the great prince which standeth for the children of thy people: and there shall be a time of trouble, such as never was since there was a nation even to that same time: and at that time thy people shall be delivered, every one that shall be found written in the book. And many of them that sleep in the dust of the earth shall awake, some to everlasting life, and some to shame and everlasting shame and everlasting contempt. And they that be wise shall shine as the brightness of the firmament; and they that turn many to righteousness as the stars forever and ever" (Daniel 12:1–3).

Some people don't believe in the Resurrection. This is true of the group called the Sadducees. They were known for their disbelief in the Resurrection. Mainly from leading families of the nation, they were high priests and powerful members of the priesthood. Before Paul revealed the mystery of the Rapture in 1 Corinthians 15:54, he discussed the resurrection body in verse 35: "But some man will say, How are the dead raised up? And with what body do they come? Thou fool, that which thou sowest is not quickened, except it die." Because the word *rapture* is not mentioned in the Bible, there are some who refuse to believe in the concept and that it is possible. We don't have to call it the Rapture; we can call it the "gathering together of the church" as in Matthew 24:31 or 2 Thessalonians 2:1: "Now we beseech you, brethren, by the coming of our Lord Jesus Christ, and by our gathering together unto him." We can call it "the catching away of the saints" (see 1 Thessalonians 4:17); "our changing" (see 2 Corinthians 3:18); or "the reimaging" (see Colossians 3:10). Whatever you choose to call it, this is only the beginning. There is more yet to come, including a time such as has never been before nor shall there ever be, the long awaited and greatest battle in all of human history, and the person commonly called the Antichrist. The most anticipated figure other than Jesus Christ in Scripture will come on the scene suddenly and pose as a false christ or a false messiah. Let us take a closer look into what this figure will be like.

Chapter Three
False Christs

Since the Creation, God has always planned to send a Savior into the world. Someone whom the world would follow and who would save the world from inevitable destruction and eternal damnation. That person was promised specifically to come through the nation of Israel. It was promised to Abraham, Isaac, and Jacob. It was promised to David that a descendant would come through his lineage who would sit on his throne forever. Judah was the tribe through which this king would come. Our very first Bible prophecy is found in Genesis 3:15. It is the first prophecy of the coming Messiah: "And I will put enmity between thee and the woman, and between thy seed and her seed; it shall bruise thy head, and thou shall bruise his heel." Here God promises a Redeemer from the offspring of the woman. Just as she had part in the fall of man, she will be allowed to participate in bringing the Messiah into the earth, to have a part in the redemption of man. This mission—known as the "desire of women"—is talked about in the books of Daniel and Revelation. "The "desire of women" was to give birth to the Messiah, to be the one chosen by God to bring forth God. This prophetic mission was fulfilled through the Virgin Mary as described in the Gospel writings of Luke and Matthew.

From the first prophecy came the others concerning the coming of the Messiah. All prophecy is centered on Jesus Christ. If a given prophecy does not concern Jesus and the advance of his kingdom, including the growth and expansion of the church and the good of Israel and the world, then we must ask ourselves if the prophecy given and the one who spoke it are really from God. True prophecy is not about us getting a new house, a new car, getting rich, or being tremendously blessed for our own selfish reasons. If it does not glorify God by exalting Jesus, then it is not from God. From Genesis to Revelation, the Bible is filled with true prophecy, authentic prophecy, and all of it is about the person of Jesus Christ and speaks of his advents (First and Second Coming) here on earth. Since Jesus is the focus of Bible prophecy and has been promised by God as Redeemer, Savior, and Deliverer, Satan has made many attempts to thwart the plan of God by first attempting to stop Christ from being birthed into the world. When prophecy was voiced that a deliverer would come to free the Hebrew people in Egypt who were under Egyptian oppression by Pharaoh, an order went out to kill all male children who were two years old and under. In the New Testament we see King Herod repeating this same type of evil: "Then Herod, when he saw that he was deceived by the wise men, was exceedingly angry; and he sent forth and put to death all the male children who were in Bethlehem and in all its districts, from two years old and under, according to the time which he had determined from the wise men" (Matthew 2:16 NKJV).

The three monotheistic religions of Christianity, Judaism, and Islam all have something in common: similar origins. They all have their roots in Abraham, the father of faith mentioned in the Bible. God used Abraham to bring forth the nation of Israel, through which he promised that all the nations of the earth would be blessed. Abraham's first son born to him was Ishmael, but he wasn't the one through whom God would bless the entire world. Isaac, his second son, the son of promise, continued the lineage leading up to the nation of Israel through Jacob (whose name was changed to Israel after wrestling with God). Descendants of Jacob's fraternal twin, Esau, were the Edomites (Arabs). This is where we get the Jewish faith from and where Christian faith has its beginnings. These three religions—Islam, Judaism, and Christianity—all have a belief in a savior. Muslims (followers of Islam) are looking for what they call the Mahdi (the enlightened one), Jews (followers of Judaism from the whole of the twelve tribes of Israel and converts) are looking for what they call the Messiah (Mashiah); and Christians (followers of Jesus Christ) are awaiting the second coming of Jesus.

Christ means "the anointed one" and is the Greek equivalent for the Hebrew word *messiah*. *Messiah* is a word that comes from the Hebrew language (Mashia), and it means "anointed by God, the sent one, or the deliverer of Israel."(Nelson's Bible Dictionary) Both words are accepted as titles. *Mahdi* means "guided one," or *Mehdi* means "one of the moon" and is also a title. The existence of Jesus as a real person is irrefutable. He is not only mentioned in the Holy Bible, but is also the central theme of the entire Old Testament as well as the New Testament. He is spoken of by the four Gospel writers, and he is well documented by the early church fathers as well as historians such as the famous Jewish historian, Josephus. He is God come in the flesh for the redemption of mankind. Christians believe that Jesus fulfilled the prophecies of Christ and is the only begotten Son of God as mentioned in the Gospel of John: 1:1"In the beginning was the Word, and the Word was with God, and the Word was God." They are waiting for the return of Jesus as promised in the Old Testament and in the New Testament 318 times. The Jews believe that Jesus existed but that he was only a prophet from God and not the Son of God. They are waiting for the Messiah to come to earth for first time. They pray daily at the Wailing Wall in expectation of the Messiah. Muslims (followers of Islam) believe that Jesus existed, and they even mention him in the Quran, their most holy book. They believe that he was a prophet but that he was not the Son of God.

The Muslims refer to Jesus as Isa Ben Maryam, which means "Jesus the son of Mary." It is interesting to note that the Muslims don't believe that Jesus was the Son of God. In Islamic eschatology, they look to the future for a man to appear that they call the Mahdi. These predictions concerning Islamic prophecies are not mentioned in their holy book, the Quran. They are part of what they call the Hadith which are sayings of their prophet

Muhammad. The Bible is the only holy book that includes prophecies (approximately 2,500 total with more than half coming to pass literally) that have been fulfilled to the letter. Islam began when Muhammad ibn Abdullah had a series of mystical visions in a cave while in Mecca. He received the visions in AD 610 but didn't start preaching until two years later in AD 612. It was believed that he could neither read nor write, so he started to recruit disciples who wrote for him. These sayings, originally written on leaves and stones, were collected and placed into the book referred to as the Quran. Muslims believe that the Quran is the last and final message of Allah to his people. Allah is the title of God to Muslims. They believe in the Torah and the Gospels, but they believe that it has been tampered with or misinterpreted by Christians and Jews. A more accurate statement would be that they believe that the Torah and the Gospels have been corrupted.

Why are Islam and Islamic beliefs of importance during the end times? Because Islam will be the eighth and final world power (the last three and a half years of the Tribulation) before the return of Jesus Christ. In Islamic prophecy, the Mahdi—Muhammad al-Mahdi—is believed to be the last of the Twelve Imams. Muhammad al-Mahdi was born in 869 CE and was hidden by God at the age of five in 874 CE. They believe he is still alive in occultation awaiting the time when God will allow his return. Muslims believe that he will fill the world with justice and fairness, and that he will be a forerunner to Jesus' Islamic rule on earth. They believe that he will come at least seven years (Tribulation) before the return of Jesus. (Yes, they believe that Jesus will return.) They teach that Jesus will come back to convert the world to Islam and to rule with the Mahdi. But before he can share rule with the Mahdi, they say that he has to tell the world that he lied about being the Son of God and that God has no Son. First, the Bible says in Romans 3:4 "Let God be true, but every man a liar." Secondly, Jesus is the truth and the life; every word that Jesus spoke prophetically has come to pass literally or will be fulfilled exactly as prophesied in the future. Thirdly, Jesus is God and does not have to accompany anyone to establish peace in the earth. Peace through Jesus has already been prophesied in the Word of God. Jesus is the ultimate superhero and does not need a sidekick.

How does someone who is looking for truth choose which faith to follow in a world so filled with failing hope? All one would have to do is hear the message that is being preached by the group in question and understand and interpret the message correctly. To do that properly, we need to examine the messenger, the one who delivers the message. The messenger can be viewed as the prophet. A prophet is a person who delivers divine messages or foretells the future. If a prophet gives unstable, inaccurate, or unreliable messages, or even predicts events that do not come to pass, then that person is a false prophet. False prophets can be categorized into three sorts: a person who worships false gods and serves idols, a person who falsely claims to receive from God, and a person who has wandered from the truth and has ceased being a true prophet. False prophets can be detected by the fruit that they bear.

Matthew 7:15–16 says, "Beware of false prophets, which come to you in sheep's clothing, but inwardly they are ravening wolves. You shall know them by their fruits." A true messenger of God will deliver a message of hope, will give a message of repentance to bring people back to God, will spread love and give life.

The description of the Mahdi sounds like a key figure in the last days of Bible prophecy. The Antichrist is given power to rule seven years before the return of Jesus Christ (the time of tribulation). Revelation 6:2 says, "And I saw, and behold a white horse: and he that sat on him had a bow; and a crown was given unto him: and he went forth conquering, and to conquer." The figure that comes on a white horse seems to be coming as a white knight and as a savior. This man is really what we call the Antichrist. This is the first seal, judgment, being released in the earth. God will allow man what he wants. The first time Christ came to earth he was talked about, lied about, beaten, bruised, spit on, rejected of men, and crucified, and he was God in the flesh. When he comes back for the second time, he will come in his glory. Matthew 24:30 says, "And then shall appear the sign of the Son of man in heaven: and then shall all the tribes of the earth mourn, and they shall see the Son of man coming in the clouds of heaven with power and great glory." The man who comes to imitate him will be accepted more quickly than the true Messiah was during his first advent. He is better described as the "anti-Christ." This man who comes on the white horse has a bow with no arrows, indicating the deception that follows him. He comes in as a man of peace, but he is actually the man of perdition. He comes into power on a campaign of peace, on a platform of reform. The Scripture says that he was given a crown. People helped him to get to his place of position. The crown given here is a crown of honor and position.

Some scoffers believe or teach that the figure mentioned in Revelation 6 is not the Antichrist. But they teach that the term is a reference to more than one individual or many individuals or spirits. They misinterpret and mishandle the Scripture of 1 John 2:18: "Little children, it is the last time: and as ye have heard that antichrist shall come, even now are there many antichrists; whereby we know that it is the last time." These unbelievers say that there are many antichrists. This is true in the sense that if they deny that Jesus was God that came in the flesh, then they possess the spirit of Antichrist (1 John 2:22). That's what John was referring to when he said that there are many antichrists—anyone who didn't confess Jesus as the promised Messiah, the Christ. Specifically, he was referring to the spirit that will embody the future son of perdition. *Anti* means "against." *Antichrist* means "against Christ." This includes any action that would go against everything that Christ would stand for. Denouncing the Word of God is antichrist-like; standing for abortion is antichrist-like behavior; promoting stem cell research is antichrist-like; promoting gay and lesbian marriage is antichrist-like. Not allowing the military to be filtered properly is ungodly (2 Samuel 2:18; Judges 7:4-7). Accepting and blending the worship of idols and false gods is antichrist-like.

The Bible specifically tells of the coming of a man in the end of days leading up to the return of Christ that will be possessed by Satan. Daniel 9:26–27 says, "And after threescore and two weeks shall Messiah be cut off, but not for himself: and the people of the prince that shall come shall destroy the city and the sanctuary; and the end thereof shall be with a flood, and unto the end of the war desolations are determined. And he shall confirm a covenant with many for one week; and in the midst of the week he shall cause the sacrifice and the oblation to cease, and for the overspreading of abominations he shall make it desolate, even until the consummation, and that determined shall be poured upon the desolate." The "prince that shall come" who is being spoken of here is the Antichrist. It is only one man that this verse is speaking of and not several and not many spirits. "He" is a personal pronoun and refers to the one last mentioned. "He" also speaks of one, not several.

Another passage that talks about the coming Antichrist is Revelation 13. In Revelation 13 is John's vision of future events, and in verse one he begins with a vision of the coming Antichrist: "And I stood upon the sand of the sea, and saw a beast rise up out of the sea, having seven heads and ten horns, and upon his horns ten crowns, and upon his heads the name of blasphemy." John calls this figure a beast in the first verse of this chapter. Then he goes on to describe the characteristics of the beast in verse 2: "And the beast which I saw …" *A* ("a beast," verse 1) is an adjective and an indefinite article, and means "one": "one sort of, each; any one; connotes a thing not previously noted or recognized." (Webster's New World Dictionary) John was describing something to his audience that he wanted them to understand. *The* ("the beast," verse 2) is a definite article and it means "referring to a particular person, thing, or group; that one being spoken of already mentioned; that which is present, close, nearby, etc., as distinguished from all others viewed as remote; that one designated or identified as by a title." When the apostle John says "the," he is identifying a specific person or thing. He calls this person a beast. This same person is identified as the Antichrist in 1 John 2. John most definitely is speaking of a future figure that will come and be powered by Satan and will mock Christ, becoming the Antichrist. He will be the ultimate and final false christ and false messiah.

Chapter Four
Is There Still Hope?

Revelation 7:5 says, "After this I beheld, and, lo a great multitude, which no man could number, of all nations and kindreds, and people, and tongues, stood before the throne, and before the lamb clothed with white robes, and palms in their hands." This passage shows that there is hope after the Tribulation period starts. The enemy would like for us to think that once we are in our sins there is no way for us to be saved and make it into heaven. During the indignation there will be many lies that will be circulated about what is happening. Some people will be aware of the truth but will think that it is too late for them to be saved from eternal judgment. As long as they did not receive the mark of the beast, or worship the beast or his image, then they can still be saved.

What do you do when it seems as if all hope is lost? Your loved ones have left you here. The world is in complete chaos, or at least it appears that way for a short while until the charismatic one brings everyone together. But even then, it still seems as if something else is wrong or something is missing. It appears that the atmosphere has changed. People appear to be brainwashed in a sense. Nobody is asking questions that lead to the truth. Everyone just accepts what he or she is being told. The economy is changing, crime has risen despite our technological advances, and sickness is a constant issue. Where did it all originate? And why do people have to experience all of these horrible things? What do you do when you don't know what to do?

The book of Genesis teaches us that in the beginning the world was without form and void. Some scholars believe that the world was empty and unshaped because of Satan being cast down to the earth. Jesus says in Luke 10:1, "I beheld Satan as lightning being cast down to earth." Some believe that before Satan was cast down to earth, the earth was made whole as God intended the world to be. There is a theory called the Gap theory that says in between Genesis 1:1 and Genesis 1:2 is the fall of Satan. That's why the Bible says that the earth was without form and void. The Hebrew word for *was* translates "became without form and void." God does not create something empty and without shape. When the world was empty and unformed, it was as if there was no use for it. It was as if there was no hope for the earth. It was covered totally with water, it was dark, and there were no living inhabitants to occupy it. But then all of a sudden, something happened. Genesis 1:3 says, "And the Spirit of God moved upon the face of the deep, And God said, Let there be light: and there was light." Just when everything appeared to be hopeless, when it seemed as though there was no hope in sight, in stepped God, who moved and shined light on the entire world.

The battle cannot always be seen with our physical eyes, but with our spiritual sight. There is a battle going on in the spirit realm that we cannot see with our natural eyes. For instance, 2 Kings 6:17 says, "And Elisha prayed, and said, Lord, I pray thee, open his eyes, that he may see. And the Lord opened the eyes of the young man; and he saw: and, behold, the mountain was full of horses and chariots of fire round about Elisha." The servant of the man of God was an assistant to Elisha. When he went out early in the morning, he discovered that the king of Syria had sent his army to surround the city to capture Elisha because the king was informed that Elisha was advising Israel's king about information regarding the king of Syria's strategic plans against Israel. The young servant was scared because of the army that surrounded the city. He asked Elisha, What are we going to do? The first thing that Elisha said to the young man was "fear not." He did not want him to have fear, because fear can cripple any hope that one may have. Elisha prayed that God would open the eyes of the young man. When God did, he was able to see an army of angelic host great and mighty. The army was so big that it says that the mountain was full of horses and chariots of fire. "What shall we then say to these things? If God be for us, who can be against us?" (Romans 8:31). The horses and chariots of fire were ready to destroy the army of the king of Syria. They would have protected the man of God at all cost.

Hope is defined as "earnest expectation; the feeling that what is wanted can be had or that events will turn out for the best; a person or thing in which expectations are centered; to look forward to with desire and reasonable confidence; to believe, desire, or trust; a feeling that what is wanted will happen; desire accompanied by expectation; to want and expect; to trust or rely."(Nelson's Bible Dictionary) Psalms 31:24 says, "Be of good courage, and he shall strengthen your heart, all ye that hope in the Lord." God has on multiple occasions fulfilled the expectations of his people. If one doesn't have hope in anything, then he has given up on everything. The Bible says that "hope deferred maketh the heart sick: but when the desire cometh, it is a tree of life" (Proverbs 13:12).

Titus 2:13 says, "Looking for that blessed hope and the glorious appearing of the great God and our Saviour Jesus Christ." This is believed to be a two-part event. The first part is the blessed hope. We know that the hope of the church is it's expectation that Jesus will return to take the church to heaven for the marriage of the Lamb. John 14:1–4 says, "Let not your heart be troubled: ye believe in God, believe also in me. In my Father's house are many mansions: if it were not so, I would have told you. I go to prepare a place for you. And if I go to prepare a place for you, I will come again, and receive you unto myself: that where I am, there you may be also. And whither I go ye know, and the way ye know." This is a promise given to us by Jesus himself. So the blessed hope is the expectation that Jesus will come back and take the church to heaven to be with him forever from that point on.

The second part of Titus 2:13 relates to the actual second coming of Jesus. That is when he appears to all. At the blessed hope, only the church sees him. Matthew 24:30 talks of all the tribes of the earth mourning, and seeing him, Jesus the Son of Man, coming in the clouds. Zechariah 14:4 says, "And his feet shall stand in that day upon the mount of Olives, which is before Jerusalem on the east, and the mount of Olives shall cleave in the midst thereof toward the east and toward the west, and there shall be a very great valley; and half of the mountain shall remove toward the north, and half of it toward the south." We see that the events are separate but they are classified as one event. They both concern the coming of the Lord Jesus. Because we have hope, we are in a position to petition God in times of need. There is always a need to communicate with God. Communication with God is known as prayer. Prayer with God should always look for some ray of hope. Pray without ceasing.

Not only should we pray to God, but we should also worship him. This is a practice that we have gotten away from as a country. If we pause to examine ourselves as a nation and take a look at our present moral and spiritual condition and our worldly status, we find that we are in very poor condition. Because we have turned away from God, we have in turn forfeited the blessings and riches that come along with following God. We are at war with different nations, we are on the verge of economic collapse, and we have lost our position as world leader all because over the years we have literally walked away from God. When nations stray away from God, he always gives them a chance to come back to him. God is calling us to a place of worship. According to *Webster's New World Dictionary, worship* is defined as "reverent honor and homage paid to God or a sacred personage." In its original context, it was formed from the combination of the two words *worth* and *ship*.

Worship is done in response to that which is holy and deserving of worship. It includes acts of prayer, dancing, forms of speech, song, silence, and praise. Praise is closely related to worship. It is the act of expressing approval or admiration, commendation, laudation. It is the offering of grateful homage in words or song.(Nelson's Bible Dictionary) We are being called back to a place of worship with God because He wants a relationship with us. And to have a relationship with God we must worship Him. Psalm 95:1 says, "O come let us sing unto the Lord: let us make a joyful noise unto Him with psalms. For the Lord is a great King above all gods. In his hand are the places of the earth: the strength of the hills is his also. The sea is his, and he made it: and his hands formed the dry land. O come, let us kneel before the Lord our maker. For He is our God; and we are the people of his pasture, and the sheep of his hand. Today if ye will hear his voice." God wants to restore us back to wholeness. For God to restore us, we must first return to Him.

When we begin to worship Him again, we will once again be blessed as a nation. Our economy will begin to flourish, our military will continue to mount victory after victory in battle, our streets will become safe again, and many numerous blessings will come along with right relationship and constant communion with God. Once we gain fellowship with God through prayer, praise, and worship, we have to remain faithful to Him even when things don't seem as if they are working toward our good. Romans 8:28 says, "And we know that all things work together for good to them that love God, to them who are the called according to his purpose." So is there still hope? No matter what it looks like, remember that there is still hope. All you have to do is put your faith in God and He will deliver you.

Chapter Five
Stand Fast

Second Thessalonians 2: 1–4, 13–17 says, "Now we beseech you, brethren, by the coming of our Lord Jesus Christ, and by our gathering together unto him, That you be not soon shaken in mind, or be troubled, neither by spirit, nor by word, nor by letter as from us, as that day of Christ is at hand. Let no man deceive you by any means for that day shall not come, except there come a falling away first, and that man of sin be revealed, the son of perdition. Who opposeth and exalted himself above all that is called God, or that is worshipped; so that he as God sitteth in the temple of God shewing himself that he is God. … But we are bound to give thanks always to God for you, brethren beloved of the Lord, because God hath from the beginning chosen you to salvation through sanctification of the Spirit and belief of the truth: Whereunto he called you by our gospel, to the obtaining of the glory of our Lord Jesus Christ. Therefore, brethren, stand fast, and hold the traditions which ye have been taught, whether by word, or our epistle. Now our Lord Jesus Christ himself, and God, even our Father, which hath loved us, and hath given us everlasting consolation and good hope through grace, Comfort your hearts, and establish you in every good word and work."

As members of the church, as children of Issachar, or men of understanding, we have to understand the times that we live in. According to Jewish custom, we are in what is called a Sabbath year. The year 2010 to 2011 is called a year of Jubilee (forty-ninth to fiftieth year). And seven Sabbaths from now will be the next Jubilee year (the fiftieth year). It is important to note that we are living in what we call the last days. When we look at the present condition of our society, we notice the rising of violent crime, the increase of immorality, the skyrocketing of gas prices, and the cost-of-living expenses spinning out of control. We notice an obvious apostasy or a turning away from God. Second Timothy 3:1 says, "This know also, that in the last days perilous times shall come. For men shall be lovers of their own selves, covetous, boasters, proud, blasphemers, disobedient to parents, unthankful, unholy. Without natural affection, trucebreakers, false accusers, incontinent, fierce, despisers of those that are good, Traitors, heady, high minded, lovers of pleasures more than lovers of God. Having a form of godliness, but denying the power thereof: from such turn away." From this description we are definitely living in the last days.

It wasn't until they took prayer out of the schools that we began to see the number of school shootings and killings increase. It wasn't until they took prayer out of the schools that we began to see our children's grades and test scores drop. It wasn't until they took prayer out of the schools that we began to see the drop-out rates soar. It wasn't until they started to ban biblical Scripture and symbols like the Ten Commandments from the courtrooms that we began to see injustice in our court systems. The fact is that we see the nation and even the entire world getting further and further from the Word of God.

The apostle Paul wrote the letters to the Thessalonians, the first of thirteen letters (or fourteen if we assign the book of Hebrews to him). The first letter confirms these young disciples in fundamental truths already taught to them, to exhort them to continue in holiness and give comfort concerning those who passed away in the faith. The second letter he wrote to instruct them concerning the Day of the Lord. They were being told that they had missed the Lord. He wanted this young group to be firm in the things that they had been taught. Apparently, someone had forged Paul's name to a letter that he did not pen. False teachers had come into the church and had begun to teach the church false doctrines. This fake letter was being circulated and had begun to trouble these young disciples. They were challenged because the letter shifted in its position on the coming of Christ. Paul explained in his letter that there must first come a falling away, then the man of sin would be revealed. "Falling away" means that many would turn away from the faith and that many in the faith would defect in their faith.

Errors and mistakes tend to weaken one's faith. The pattern of our thinking can lead our faith to frailty and then total dissipation. Some religions and cults teach that Jesus was only a prophet; some teach that he is the same as Michael the archangel. Some teach that he didn't rise from the dead at all. Some don't believe that he actually lived, that the stories were fabricated. That is why it is important that we should be submitted to a church and its leaders that we may learn the Word of God in a systematic environment. We must not mix the Word of God with any other religion or doctrine. We must not and we cannot.

We must not acquiesce the atheist, we must not become baffled with Buddhism, we must not get confused by Confucius, and we must not become dumbfounded with Darwinism. We must not ever equate with evolution; we must not be hindered by Hinduism. We cannot joke with the Jehovah's Witnesses; we must not kid around with the Cabalists. We must not mix beliefs with the Muslims. We must not find spiritual nourishment from the Nation. We must not be fooled with the Pharisees; we cannot sample the bread of the Sadducees because they didn't believe in the Resurrection and that is "sad you see." We must not be sucked in by the Scientologists. All of these belief systems contain some wisdom and have nuggets for living, but they are incomplete for life. John 10:10 says, "The thief cometh not, but to steal, and to kill, and to destroy: I am come that they might have life and that they might have it more abundantly." Jesus said, "I am the way, the truth, and the life, no man cometh to the Father but by me."

Part of my assignment is to come to encourage the people to stand fast. Don't be a part of the group that loses faith. Don't be a part of the group that falls away. Stand firm in your belief of what you have been taught from the Holy Scriptures from your youth. Stand on the Word when things seem unstable. Second Peter 2:9 says, "The Lord is not slack concerning his promise, as some men count slackness; but is longsuffering to us-ward, not willing that any should perish, but that all should come to repentance." I'm here to tell you that it is not too late. You have not missed God. If you are not a part of the faith you can sign up today. It doesn't matter what you have done. It doesn't matter why you are here. Just ask God to forgive you for the things that you have done. The Word says in Romans 10:9, "That if you confess with thy mouth the Lord Jesus, and shalt believe in thine heart that God hath raised him from the dead, thou shalt be saved." Once you have grabbed on to the faith, don't let go. Stand fast.

Joseph had remained in prison for thirteen years altogether—and for a crime that he didn't commit. He always remained faithful to God. His character was one of the purest in biblical history. He allowed no temptation to affect his high morality, no adversity to depress him, no power or position to make him proud; and he allowed no calamity to shake his faith. God elevated him to the keeper of the prison. While there, He was able to interpret the dreams of two men, both of which came to pass. Afterward, he told the butler to remember him once he got out of prison, but it was two full years before Joseph was released. That year was a Jubilee year. The significance of the Jubilee year was that it was a year of release when all who were in the faith were released from their bondage. If they were slaves, they were freed from slavery. If they owned land but leased it out to pay debt, the land was released and given back to them. Everything that they had before they were imprisoned was restored unto them fully.

Chapter Six

Trust in Him

"Some trust in chariots, and some in horses: but we will remember the name of the Lord our God" (Psalm 20:7). In such uncertain times as these, people tend to depend on things like family, friends, government, jobs, doctors, lawyers, lottery, themselves, etc. Psalm 20 is a prayer in which David relays the prayers of the people for his victory in battle in verses 1–5. His own beliefs are voiced in verse 7. The last two verses (8 and 9) are concluded by reiterating the prayer of the people. David had attained the kingship of Judah and all of Israel. But it did not happen instantaneously. It took more than fifteen years for David to become king of Israel after receiving the prophecy and after being anointed king by the prophet Samuel.

David, whose name means "beloved" was raised in Bethlehem and became the second king of the United Kingdom of Israel. He was the youngest son of Jesse, but not the least important. He was anointed by Samuel the prophet in 1 Samuel 16:13: "Then Samuel took the horn of oil, and anointed him in the midst of his brethren; and the Spirit of the Lord came upon David from that day forward, so Samuel rose up, and went to Ramah." When he took the throne, it was almost sixteen years later. This should provide us with a biblical example of patience. Some of us today when we receive a prophetic utterance concerning ourselves, are in such a hurry to have the prophecy come to pass. We even attempt to help God bring the vision to fruition. To wait sixteen days, let alone sixteen years, for fulfillment of a prophecy to materialize for some of us is unimaginable. For David it was not an issue. David had a lot of time on his hands from the time that he received the prophecy that he would become king until the time when he took the throne, but he did not become restless.

Before becoming king, David was the keeper of his father's sheep. He was a shepherd from the early stages of his life so he had a shepherd's heart. A shepherd has a special relationship with his sheep. Sheep depend on shepherds for everything. They depend on them to lead them to water and pasture. They depend on shepherds to fight off wild animals. Shepherds anoint their sheep's faces for when they are grazing in pastures and a snake nips them on the nose so that the venom and the bite just slide off. Sheep naturally trust their shepherds. Shepherds know their sheep by name, and sheep recognize the voice of their masters. Sheep are models of submissiveness. Jesus demonstrated his submissiveness with purity and trustful obedience. John 1:29–30 calls Jesus the Lamb of God: "The next day John saw Jesus coming toward him and said, 'Behold, the Lamb of God who takes away the sin of the world.' Again, the next day, John stood with two other disciples. And looking at Jesus as He walked, he said, 'Behold the Lamb of God.'"

In Psalm 23 David wrote about the nature of the relationship between sheep and shepherd. This psalm says, "The Lord is my shepherd ; I shall not want. He maketh me to lie down in green pastures: he leadeth me beside the still waters. He restoreth my soul: he leadeth me in the paths of righteousness for his name's sake. Yea, though I walk through the valley of the shadow of death, I will fear no evil: for thou art with me; thy rod and thy staff they comfort me. Thou preparest a table before me in the presence of mine enemies: thou anointest my head with oil; my cup runneth over. Surely goodness and mercy shall follow me all the days of my life: and I will dwell in the house of the Lord forever." This is one of the most popular psalms. It is often quoted but not always fully understood by its readers. This psalm pictures the Lord as leader, guide, protector, provider, redeemer, savior, comforter, and companion.

The Lord is compared to a shepherd for his people, giving His sheep everything that they need and desire, withholding no good thing from them. He knows what is best for us and causes us to be blessed by making us to rest in fruitful places. He takes us to quiet, peaceful places free from the vices of the enemy where our thirst is quenched and where we rest in his salvation. He guides us according to his goodness only because

32

he is good and his name is great. We travel with danger lurking around every corner, but we place our trust in the Lord because he travels with us. He reassures us with his Word. Before us are laid the blessings and the provision of the Lord while our adversaries view us with envy. God blesses us and overflows our vats. There is no doubt that his unmerited favor and his tenderness will not leave us but will cling to us tightly for as long as we shall live. And we have an everlasting dwelling place in heaven with the Lord.

Abraham also put his trust in the Lord according to Scripture. In Genesis 12:1, God urged Abram (whose name was later changed to Abraham) to leave the land of his father and go to a land that he would show to him, a land flowing with milk and honey. Abraham prayed to God that He would establish Abraham's seed forever and that they would not go astray from God's way. The idolatry of Abraham's day and of his people was well understood by Abraham. God heard Abraham's heart and commanded him to leave his homeland and journey to a new place. Genesis 12:1 says, "Now the Lord had said unto Abram, Get thee out of thy country, and from thy kindred, and from thy father's house, unto a land that I will shew thee: And I will make of thee a great nation, and I will bless thee, and make thy name great, and thou shalt be a blessing: And I will bless thee, and curse him that curseth thee: and in thee shall all families of the earth be blessed. So Abram departed, as the Lord had spoken unto him." After receiving the instruction of the Lord, Abraham did just as the Lord asked. Unlike some who are put in the same situation might do, Abraham didn't stop God and ask for specific information. He didn't even ask what direction God wanted him to travel in, which indicates that he allowed God's Spirit to guide him for every move that he made. He didn't ask God what the blessings would be. He didn't complain to God about how rough the journey would be. He simply did as the Lord had outlined and planned for his life.

"A man after God's own heart," "a friend of God," and "a just and perfect man": these describe just a few men who chose to put their trust in God. The Bible is full of men and women of God who placed faith in the Lord. Hebrews 11 gives us a list of heroes of faith. A hall of fame, so to speak, of individuals who were faith walkers: Abel and his sacrifice. Enoch in his walk. Noah in his preparation. Abraham in his obedience. Sara and her strength. Isaac and his blessing. Jacob in his worship. Joseph

33

and his commandment. Moses and his affliction. The people of God in their deliverance. The walls of Jericho and their tumbling. Rahab and her belief. And not to mention Gideon, and Barak, and Samson, and Jephthah, and David, and Samuel, and the prophets.

Paul also trusted fully in the Lord. Paul called himself a "Hebrew of the Hebrews" (Philippians 3:5). Born in Tarsus, he was also brought up in Jerusalem and studied at the feet of Gamaliel, the most sought-after rabbi of his day. His passion and zeal for the law far surpassed that of his fellow students. The rise of Christianity and its claim that Jesus, who was just condemned by Jewish officials and crucified by Roman authorities, was the promised Messiah threatened Paul and his mission to preserve Jewish law. He then began to persecute the Christians intensely. He was present at the stoning of Stephen in the book of Acts. Chapter 8:3 says, "As for Saul, he made havoc of the church, entering into every house, and haling men and women committed them to prison." (Saul is Paul's Jewish name.) Paul received letters from the high priest to go to Damascus with the assignment of persecuting the church. Before the Lord gave him his assignment, the apostle Paul, thinking he was in the will of God, was actually in opposition to the will of God. It was here on his mission to Damascus that he was struck by God, and after being knocked off his horse and blinded, he was converted by God. God instructed a disciple named Ananias to seek Saul at the house of Judas, where he would find Saul praying. Then he was to lay hands on Saul and Saul would be healed of his blindness.

Ananias was told by God that Paul would suffer great things for His name's sake. Paul himself spoke of some of the things that he suffered in 2 Corinthians 11:23–27: "Are they ministers of Christ? (I speak as a fool) I am more; in labours more abundant, in stripes above measures, in prisons more frequent, in deaths oft. Of the Jews five times received I forty stripes save one. Thrice was I beaten with rods, once was I stoned, thrice I suffered shipwreck, a night and a day I have been in the deep. In journeyings often, in perils of waters, in perils of robbers, in perils by mine own countrymen, in perils by the heathen, in perils in the city, in perils in the wilderness, in perils in the sea, in perils among false brethren; In weariness and painfulness, in watchings often, in hunger and thirst, in fastings often, in cold and nakedness." Paul was in constant danger after he accepted Christ as Lord and Savior, but he did not allow those dangers to altar his faith. In Romans 8:35 he says, "Who shall separate us from the love of Christ? shall tribulation, or distress, or persecution, or famine, or nakedness, or peril, or sword?" Verse 38 says, "For I am persuaded, that neither death, nor life, nor angels, nor principalities, nor powers, nor things present, nor things to come, Nor height, nor depth, nor any other creature, shall be able to separate us from the love of God, which is in Christ Jesus our Lord." For Paul there was no turning back.

Today, we don't seem to be as trusting as some of the early matriarchs and patriarchs of the Bible. From the first man Adam to the apostle John of Revelation, each man or women of the Bible trusted God and moved with faith and was rewarded with God's glory. Over the past six thousand years, technological advances have caused us to leave faith in God and trust things like man-made devices and man's increased knowledge in fields like medicine, farming, agriculture, architecture, psychology, etc. We would rather spend time on our computer or our mobile devices and televisions than spend time praying or studying the Word of God. In the pages of the Bible there are over 2,500 prophecies from the time of inception, and over half of those prophecies have come to fulfillment to the exact letter just as the prophets predicted. To put trust in God is wise based on the 100-percent track record of God's Word.

Chapter Seven
Point of No Return

"And the Lord said unto him, Therefore whosoever slayeth Cain, vengeance shall be taken on him sevenfold. And the Lord set a mark upon Cain, lest any finding him should kill him." (Genesis 4:15) Cain and Able were the first children mentioned in the Bible who were from Adam and Eve. Cain was a tiller of the ground, and Abel was a keeper of the sheep. Cain killed his brother Abel out of jealousy because God accepted Abel's offering but rejected Cain's offering. When asked about his brother's whereabouts by God, Cain lied and replied, "Am I my brother's keeper?" (Genesis 4:9)God knew exactly what Cain did to his brother Abel; He wanted Cain to confess. God told Cain that if he did right he would be accepted. He wanted Cain to control sin, not for sin to control him. Since Cain had sinned, there had to be punishment for the sin that he committed. So God did not allow the ground to yield any strength to Cain. Adam in his sin had the ground cursed by God, forcing Adam to toil for it to produce. Cain (the third to be cursed by God), who had become a tiller of the ground by trade, was cursed even further by God; the ground would not even yield its strength to him. Whatever he attempted to do would not produce. But God still allowed him to live.

In addition to the ground not yielding to him, for the murder of his brother, Cain was also driven out from the presence of the Lord. Just like Adam and Eve were banned from the Garden of Eden, so we see Cain being pushed even further away from a sinless God. Cain was the first one to be marked by God. God was the first to place a mark on His own. This particular mark that God placed on Cain was not to identify Cain as a criminal, but it was to protect Cain from anyone taking vengeance on him for slaying his brother Abel. Who would want to slay Cain for the murder of Abel? It would be the other siblings of Cain and Abel. Genesis 5:4 says, "After he begat Seth, the days of Adam were eight hundred years; and he had sons and daughters." The siblings of the first two brothers would want to avenge the death of Abel. Included in this five-fold punishment by God to Cain was that the ground would not yield to him, he was driven out from God's presence, he was hidden from the face of the Lord, he would be a fugitive and a vagabond in the earth, and he would be killed by anyone who found him. He showed no remorse or sorrow for the crime that he had committed.

It is unfortunate that there are similarities between Cain and his situation in his time, and the young men and women in our day. Young men get involved in a life of crime and become unproductive in the workforce, thus leaving the responsibility of providing for the family on the female, who consciously chooses as a mate a criminal or thug, possibly for some false sense of security. Cain wasn't too concerned about the fact that the ground would not yield to him; he wasn't worried about being driven out of his dwelling place. He didn't seem bothered by the fact that he would not be in the presence of the Lord or that he would be running the rest of his life. He was worried about being killed by one of his siblings for killing his brother. Though he did it to someone else, he didn't want anyone to do it to him. The golden rule in almost every culture is "do unto others as you would have them do unto you." If he was more concerned about maintaining his relationship with God, maybe this unfortunate string of events could have been avoided.

It is true that God is a gracious and forgiving God. He is love, and He loves His human creation. He is longsuffering, merciful, and caring. Even with these tender characteristics, if man violates God's law past a certain point, there is no coming back. God is open to receive all of his human creation into eternal life with him, but he knows that all will not accept this free gift of salvation. Why would people not be willing to live free from sin, free of pain, free of strife, free of struggle, free from stress, free of crime, free of suffering? Maybe because they feel that what they have is better than anything else that will be or exist. Maybe because some people would rather have gratification here and now, not fully understanding the end result. We want to do what we want to without any rules or supervision, especially by God—some entity that we cannot see. We want the benefits of a relationship with God without being held accountable to God. We choose whom we will follow by our actions and inactions. If we do wrong, then we have chosen to follow Satan and the ungodly line of Cain. Satan always mimics God in everything that he does. Satan attempts to mark those who follow him. Those who choose to obey God and accept Jesus Christ as Lord will benefit by spending eternity with Him.

The nation of Israel believed that because they were in covenant with God they would always enjoy the benefits from that relationship. But the covenant was conditional. They had to follow God, His laws and commands. Because of constant disobedience, they were punished by God. God allowed foreign nations to invade and scatter Israel and to defeat and ban Judah from Jerusalem and to take them captive, destroying their temple and scattering their tribes. God would always bring His people back to remembrance of Him and His covenant promises. But there is a point that cannot be crossed by anyone. If it is, then there is no coming back from that point. So what exactly is the point of no return? Let's examine what the Word of God teaches us.

"And the third angel followed them, saying with a loud voice, If any man worship the beast and his image, and receive his mark in his forehead, or in his hand, The same shall drink of the wine of the wrath of God, which is poured out without mixture into the cup of his indignation; and he shall be tormented with fire and brimstone in the presence of the holy angels, and in the presence of the Lamb" (Revelation 14:9–10). Whoever accepts the mark of the Beast shall suffer God's wrath. Notice the fire and brimstone of hell that is mentioned here. The worst part is not the burning in hell, but being viewed by Jesus Christ and the holy angels for all of eternity. Isaiah 66:24 also describes in the Millennium the ability to look on those who are in hell by everyone who comes to worship before the Lord: "And they shall go forth, and look upon the carcases of the men that have transgressed against me: for their worm shall not die, neither shall their fire be quenched; and they shall be an abhorring unto all flesh." Verse 11 of Revelation 14 makes clear the length of the torture of those who accept the mark of the Beast: "And the smoke of their torment ascendeth up forever and ever: and they have no rest, day nor night, who worship the beast and his image, and whosoever receiveth the mark of his name."

The passage in Revelation 14:9 is the third announcement by one of three angels in the fourteenth chapter of Revelation. The third angel preaches the doom of those who worship the Beast. The Beast is a three-pronged satanic system (political, economic, and religious) centered on the person of and led by the Antichrist. The way that one worships the Beast is described in this same passage of Scripture. All one would have to do is to accept the mark. The mark is the mark of the Beast. In this case the mark is the number of the Beast, the name of the Beast, or the mark itself. The number can be identified because it is the number of a man as described in Revelation 13:18: "Here is wisdom. Let him that hath understanding count the number of the beast: for it is the number of a man; and his number is Six hundred threescore and six." The mark is not the number 666, but it is the numerical value of six hundred sixty-six. It can be seen as a brand of a company or its logo.

Most companies have a symbol or a sign that is identifiable with that company. McDonald's has the golden arch; Nike has the swoosh symbol; Mercedes has its signature emblem, a circle with three equally distant lines. This "company" makes people its product and uses the number of man as its sign. A mark identifies something; it shows ownership of a thing. A symbol is a sign that the product it is on belongs to a certain person, group, or company. The mark in Revelation points to the owner or the manufacturer of the mark, which is the product of the Antichrist. The mark is a counterfeit of the seal of the living God. Those who accept the mark are being sealed with the seal of approval of the Antichrist. Once the mark has been accepted by an individual and applied, he or she is marked forever. There is no coming back after receiving the mark. You can't burn it off; you can't cut it off; you can't break it off; you can't cover it up. Once it is received, there is no giving it back.

The benefits of receiving the seal are that the recipients of the seal would be able to buy and sell freely. Revelation 13:16–17 teaches us that the second Beast caused people from all classes and walks of life to receive a mark in their forehead or their right hand. It is connected with the economy and its restructured system. The restructure obviously has come because of a worldwide economic collapse. Once God receives his people to Himself, the world will indeed collapse economically. Then there will be a need to restructure because a significant number of people will go missing from an already failing economy. Many mortgages will go unpaid, as well as car notes, insurance policies, etc. Employers will lose employees and will be devastated in their businesses and trying to replace those who have vanished. In this event the first Beast has been creative in devising a system that the entire world embraces, and the second Beast causes them all to receive the symbol of the system. After the salt of the earth is removed, the entire world goes into a frenzy and everything nearly collapses. But not before the Antichrist brings all the nations together to accept this system.

The mark of the Beast is first mentioned in chapter 13 of Revelation. Verse 17 speaks of three different types of the mark: the mark itself, the name of the Beast, and the number of his name. This indicates that the mark will not be easy to detect and will be disguised. Earlier, I mentioned that one of the brands of the mark will be the number of man. And it is the numerical value of the Beast's name not the three-digit numeral 666. One would have to have knowledge in Hebraic numerology. And it would most likely be the Hebrew system of numerology called gematria. Also, because some portions of the book of Revelation are not in chronological order—the information on the Beast and his mark being one example—it is unclear and we are unaware at what juncture the mark would be introduced to the world. It is likely that it will be enforced during the second half of the Tribulation. Whatever point it is introduced, if the mark is accepted, there can be no coming back.

"Verily I say unto you, All sins shall be forgiven unto the sons of men, and blasphemies wherewith soever they shall blaspheme: But he that shall blaspheme against the Holy Ghost hath never forgiveness, but is in danger of eternal damnation" (Mark 3:28–29). Not only is accepting the mark of the Beast a way of no return, but blaspheming the Holy Ghost is a one-way ticket as well. To *blaspheme* means "to speak evil of; to speak irreverently or profanely of or to (God or sacred things); to curse or revile."(Webster's New World Dictionary) The Holy Ghost is the most misunderstood member of the triune Being. He is the very essence of God. To blaspheme the Holy Ghost is to speak evil of Him and God in His entirety. If one does this forbidden act, then he or she then also crossed over to a point of no return.

Chapter Eight

Last Things

We previously discussed that there are seven major events that surround the second coming of Jesus Christ back to earth: the Rapture, Tribulation, Second Coming, Battle of Armageddon, and millennial reign of Christ, Great White Throne Judgment, and the Eternal State. These seven events can be viewed collectively as the Day of the Lord. The Day of the Lord is a series of events that have yet to take place or come to pass. The Bible contained approximately 2,500 prophecies at the time that it was written. More than half of these prophecies are already fulfilled literally. If these prophecies have been fulfilled literally, then we must come to the same conclusion about the remaining prophecies. We must be careful not to misinterpret allegorical Scriptures, but we must study to determine the meaning. We must not spiritualize Scripture as if the writer meant his prophecies in a spiritual, rather than a literal, sense. All prophecy concerns Jesus Christ. Every prophecy that is foretold in our Bible concerning the first advent of Jesus Christ has come to pass in the literal sense, so we have to conclude that the prophecies of his second advent will also. The last seven major events of Bible prophecy are about his coming back literally to earth to rule and reign.

God truly has a plan for his redemption of man and the world. The first part of that plan was performed when Christ came and died on the cross for the sin of man. That was only the first portion of God's plan. God always intended for Christ to return to earth to complete the plan of redemption that God had ordained from the foundation of the earth and what was started way back on Calvary. There are seven major events that surround the second coming of our Lord and Savior Jesus Christ. The event that starts the seven events is known as the rapture of the church, which we have discussed in some detail. The Rapture is first on God's prophetic timetable. This is only the beginning of these events surrounding the second advent of our Lord Jesus Christ. The Bible says in Matthew 24:36, "But of that day and hour knoweth no man, no, not the angels of heaven, but my Father only." Jesus admitted that even he didn't know when these things would happen. Though he did not know an exact time, I believe that if he had known, he would have given us a clue. And he did!

If we are familiar with the feasts of Israel, and if we do a Greek word study, then we can understand this verse and what it really means. The feasts of Israel were ordained by God as outlined in Leviticus 23 to prophetically fulfill in future times the plan of God for the redemption of man and the world. The Feast of Trumpets, which is synonymous with the Rapture, is the only feast that begins on the new moon. The new moon was not a full moon, but it was the sight of the beginning of the moon in its cycle. The feast could not begin until the first sliver of the moon was visible by two witnesses and then reported by the witnesses to the priest. There was a forty-eight-hour window in which the new moon could appear. That's what is meant by the phrase "no man knoweth the day nor the hour." Now the word for *know* in Strong's #1492 is IEDO (eedo) and it means "to now know" (in the present tense). So when we read the text adding "to now know," then we understand that it wasn't for that generation to know but that it could be understood by the generation that it was intended for in the distant future at that time. *This is the generation* (Matthew 24:32). I do believe that the human nature of Jesus (his humanity) did not know when the Day of the Lord would begin. However, the deity of Jesus (his divinity) could have had insight to this time at the will of God. But because he was obedient in his assignment, he humbled himself as a man even unto death (Philippians. 2:7–8). At any point, once the first event begins, man can then begin to approximate the return of Jesus Christ to earth.

The next event on God's prophetic timetable after the Rapture is the tribulation period. The Tribulation is a period of intense persecution and oppression that will last for a period of seven years. Daniel 9:27 parallels this same time period. Jesus described this same time in Matthew

24:4–26. This is why man can determine approximately the date of Christ's return after the Rapture because we know that the Tribulation is seven years according to Daniel's vision. The tribulation period is a time in which God will turn his attention back to Israel and Israel will once again turn to God. God will draw the nation back to Him during this time of persecution. It will also be a time of judgment on the world for rejecting the free offer of salvation from Jesus Christ through the atoning work that he completed on the cross at Calvary. Daniel 12:1 speaks of this time of God's wrath: "And at that time shall Michael stand up, the great prince which standeth for the children of thy people: and there shall be a time of trouble, such as never was since there was a nation even to that same time: and at that time thy people shall be delivered every one that shall be found written in the book." Daniel says that this time will be a time like no other from the time of the first nation up until that future period. This passage speaks of God sending Michael the archangel to deliver His people from this coming judgment of God. Also to be delivered is everyone whose name is found written in the Book (that is the Book of Life). Daniel 9:27 confirms the length of the tribulation period: "And he shall confirm the covenant with many for one week: and in the midst of the week he shall cause the sacrifice and the oblation to cease, and for the overspreading of abominations he shall make it desolate, even until the consummation, and that determined shall be poured upon the desolate."

Next to come is the second coming of Jesus Christ. Some say that in life there are two guarantees, taxes and death. I would like to add to that statement. The one thing that we can be assured of is Christ's return to earth. The Second Coming is inevitable. It is mentioned in the New Testament alone 318 times. Acts 1:10–11 says, "And while they looked steadfastly toward heaven as he went up, behold two men stood by them in white apparel, which also said, Ye men of Galilee, why stand ye gazing up into heaven? This same Jesus, which is taken up from you into heaven shall so come in like manner as ye have seen him go into heaven." Zechariah 14:4 says, "And his feet shall stand in that day upon the mount of Olives, which is before Jerusalem on the east, and the mount of Olives shall cleave in the midst thereof toward the east and toward the west, and there shall be a very great valley; and half of the mountain shall remove toward the north, and half of it toward the south." The first time Christ came to earth he came in peace. The second time, he will come back as a conqueror. In Matthew 10:34, Jesus himself said, "Think not that I am come to send peace on earth, but a sword." Jesus came to earth as humble as a king riding to town on a donkey. In the verse mentioned, he was coming to his second advent to earth. The second time that he comes back it will be as the King, coming to conquer riding on a white horse.

In Jewish custom/history, when a king came riding a white horse, he was coming for war, coming to conquer. Revelation 6:2 says, "And I saw, and behold a white horse: and he that sat on him had a bow; and a crown was given to him: and he went forth conquering, and to conquer." This is a picture of a king being given power and conquering. But this is not Jesus coming to conquer and rule. This is a person that comes like Christ, but he is really an imposter. This is the first seal judgment of God's twenty-one total judgments (seven seal, seven trumpet, seven bowl) being released—the Antichrist coming into power. Notice this conqueror comes riding on a white horse with a bow and no arrow. This symbolizes that he was coming in peace but he was really coming as the man of sin and the son of perdition. When Jesus comes, he will be coming to conquer. Revelation 19:11 says, "And I saw heaven opened, and behold a white horse; and he that sat upon him was called Faithful and True, and in righteousness he doth judge and make war." This is the real Savior, and his name is Jesus Christ. His first order of business will be to come and do battle against the Antichrist and the armies that have united to do battle against Jerusalem. This battle is known as the Battle of Armageddon. It is the most anticipated battle of all time. Revelation 16:16 says, "And he gathered them together into a place called in the Hebrew tongue Armageddon."

The next prophetic event in God's program is the Battle of Armageddon. *Armageddon* means "mountain of Megiddo." Near the city of Megiddo at the head of the plain in Esdraelon is the site where the great Battle of Armageddon will be fought. Revelation 16:16 talks of this great, fierce battle before Christ come back to the earth. At the Battle of Armageddon all the armies of Satan come together to do battle against Israel. This is when Christ comes back to destroy Satan's army and cast him into the bottomless pit. At this point, three of the major seven events are joined together. The second coming of Christ to earth precedes the Battle of Armageddon—an event all of creation has been eagerly awaiting. When Jesus began his public ministry, he went forth preaching the gospel of the Kingdom of God (Mark 1:14): "Now after that John was put in prison, Jesus came into Galilee, preaching the gospel of the kingdom of God." The Second Coming ushers in the millennial reign of Christ.

The Millennium is a literal thousand-year period in which Christ will rule on the earth. It is a time of peace on earth, a time when there will be no fighting and no war. Some scholars (scoffers) believe that this reign is symbolic of the rule of Christ's reign in the life of the believer. Most assuredly, the Millennium is a literal one-thousand-year period in which Christ will reign on earth. This entire period will be undisturbed by Satan. This event is simultaneous with the imprisonment of Satan mentioned in Revelation. Revelation 20:2 says, "And he laid hold on the dragon, that old serpent, which is the Devil, and Satan, and bound him a thousand years." Why one thousand years? It is believed that there is a code hidden in Genesis that man has been given by God, a determined amount of time to govern himself, and the last part of that time frame would be God's governmental rule through Christ on the throne here on earth. The code suggests that man has six thousand years to rule (symbolized by the six days of Creation) and then Christ would rule the last one thousand years (the seventh day of Creation). It patterns the seven days of Creation outlined in Genesis. Second Peter 3:8 says, "But beloved, be not ignorant of this one thing, that one day is with the Lord as a thousand years, and a thousand years as one day." Psalms 90:4 says, "For a thousand years in thy sight are but as yesterday when it is past, and as a watch in the night." God told Adam in the Garden, "In the day that you eat of the tree, you shall surely die." Adam didn't die the day that he ate the fruit. He died at the age of 930, seventy years short of one thousand years. He died within the thousand years just as God said—within the "day."

The last two events on God's timetable are the Great White Throne Judgment and the Eternal State. The Great White Throne Judgment is the final in a series of judgments from God. It comes at the close of the millennial reign. It is the judgment of all people from all nations who did not receive Christ or confess faith in the God of Abraham, Isaac, and Jacob—from the beginning of time to the catching away of the saints, during the Tribulation, and the end of the age. "And I saw a great white throne, and him that sat on it, from whose face the earth and the heaven fled away; and there was found no place for them." Revelation 21:11 This judgment is one that God reserves to judge everyone who lived from Adam until this time that did not accept Jesus Christ before the gathering together of the saints and during the Tribulation. It is a judgment for those who have not accepted Christ as Lord and Savior—those who are not allowed to enter into the Lord's rest, or what is called the Millennium.

The Eternal State is a specific time designated by God in the future when God's plan for mankind and the world will be realized. Some scholars believe that this world will be destroyed and another one will be placed where the old one once sat. I believe this to be untrue. "And I saw a new heaven and a new earth for the first heaven and the first earth were passed away; and there was no more sea" (Revelation 21:1). The new heaven and the new earth is a picture of both heaven and earth that have gone through a purification process. Second Peter 3:10 says, "But the day of the Lord will come as a thief in the night; in the which the heavens shall pass away with a great noise, and the elements shall melt with fervent heat, the earth also and the works that are therein shall be burned up." The heavens and the elements that are being discussed are the stars that will fall. Some teach that the heavens and the earth will literally be destroyed by God. If we take a walk through the Scriptures we can see that they say something different from this interpretation.

Take a look at Psalms 104:5. It says, "Who laid the foundations of the earth, that it should not be removed forever." This is referring to God the Creator and His handiwork in establishing the earth at the Creation, laying the foundation. It goes on to say that there is no one or thing that can or will be able to undo what He has done and that it is established or that it shall and will be forever. The Bible says to let everything be established in the mouth of two or three witnesses. The second scriptural witness from the Bible is Ecclesiastes 1:4, and it says, "One generation passeth away, and another generation cometh: but the earth abideth for ever." The preacher in this verse talks of the frailty of humanity and how generations come and go, but it speaks of the same earth not a different one that witnesses each human being enter and exit the earth through life and death. Psalms 119:89–90 states, "For ever, O Lord, thy word is settled in heaven. Thy faithfulness is unto all generations; thou hast established the earth, and it abideth." Ephesians 3:21 says, "Unto him be glory in the church by Christ Jesus throughout all ages, world without end. Amen." Notice the second part of this verse. The author states that the world continues going on uninterrupted with no end. By studying the Scriptures we learn that in the days of Noah the Bible teaches that God destroyed the earth the first time with water. Genesis 9:11 says, "And I will establish my covenant with you; neither shall all flesh be cut off any more by the waters of a flood; neither shall there anymore be a flood to destroy the earth." So God established a covenant with man and the animals that He would not destroy flesh by a flood and that He would not destroy the earth again with a flood. In other words, man would continue to exist, and he would exist here on the earth. Here, God destroyed the earth figuratively by destroying the living things that existed on earth, yet it is the same physical planet that has always been here since the beginning of Creation. Notice verse 13: "I do set my bow in the cloud, and it shall be for a token of a covenant between me and the earth." God made a covenant with the earth!

In the Eternal State, there will be no crime, tears, death, or sin. There will be no influence of Satan. Revelation 21:4 says, "And God will wipe away all tears from their eyes; and there shall be no more death, neither sorrow, nor crying, neither shall there be any more pain: for the former things are passed away." Eternity may not be quite what we thought it would be. Growing up, I thought that when a Christian believer died, he went to heaven to be with God forever and that's where he or she got his or her long sought-after set of wings. Someone else may have thought that after we received our wings we also got a special cloud that we would sit on all day long. We were all raised with different thoughts and beliefs that are not biblically based because we were not taught the truth as it is outlined in the Bible. In eternity, we don't get wings; in eternity, we don't float on clouds; and in eternity, we don't abide in God's dwelling place forever. He has prepared a specific place for his children. John 14:2–3 says, "In my Father's house are many mansions: if it were not so, I would have told you. I go to prepare a place for you. And if I go and prepare a place for you, I will come again and receive you unto myself, that where I am there ye may be also."

"And I saw a new heaven and a new earth: for the first heaven and the first earth were passed away; and there was no more sea. And I John saw the holy city, New Jerusalem, coming down from God out of heaven, prepared as a bride adorned for her husband" (Revelation 21:1). This is the true bride of Christ, the heavenly city. The church is often referred to as the "bride of Christ," but the Scripture here shows that new Jerusalem, coming down the aisle of heaven to unite with the Bridegroom, Jesus Christ, is the bride of Christ. In the book of Genesis, Jacob met Rachel and desired her to be his bride. He committed to work for her for seven years, but instead he got Leah (the church). Genesis 29:15-30 says that "Leah was tender eyed [the church]; but Rachel was beautiful and well favoured [Israel]." Jacob agreed to work an additional seven years for Rachel. Jesus worked seven years for Israel (the first six days of Creation plus the seventh day, a day of rest). Revelation 21:10 says, "And he carried me away in the spirit to a great city, the holy Jerusalem, descending out of heaven from God." It goes on further to describe the dimensions of heaven. It is shaped like a cube, a perfectly shaped square, between 1,380 and 1,500 miles on each face. The new heaven and new earth are really fascinating and should be studied in greater detail. It is too vast a topic to discuss in this work. These are the main events concerning the second coming of Christ in short or brief detail. These events are inevitable just as the second coming of Jesus just as the Bible predicts. So in light of this information, the Bible speaks of what we should do.

Well, just in case you're still here, first of all, know that it is not too late and that you can be saved from eternal damnation. All you have to do is what it says in the Bible: "Confess with thy mouth and believe in thy heart then you shall be saved."

1. Repeat the sinner's prayer.
2. Reject the mark at all costs.
3. Stock enough dried foods and water for a long period of time.
4. Have flashlights, a radio, and batteries handy.
5. Learn to grow your own fruits/vegetables in your yard.
6. Have your Bible available and always pray.

The Bible says in Philippians 2:12, "Wherefore, my beloved, as ye have always obeyed, not as in my presence only, but now much more in my absence, work out your own salvation with fear and trembling." We are all responsible for our own salvation. If you say the sinner's prayer below, then you will be saved by the Lord and will have an eternal resting place in heaven.

Dear Lord Jesus, come into my life. I am sorry for my sins. I confess my sins to you; save me

Lord. I believe that you came and died on the cross that I may be saved. I accept your sacrifice for my sin, and I believe right now that I am saved. In Jesus' name I pray. Amen!

If you sincerely prayed this prayer for salvation, then you are saved from everlasting judgment and eternal damnation. Now you have been grafted into the family of God. Read your Bible for God's will for your life. Think of your Bible as an acronym for "Basic instructions before leaving Earth."

Lord, help us! We are moving ahead in time, coping with what has dislodged us as a whole, trying to put things in some kind of an order, not knowing what is in store for us in our time. Lord, if ever there was a time that we need you, that time is now. Lord, we are weak and have not a clue. I pray that you will guide, deliver, heal, anoint, bless, and save us. The times are rough, and we do need you. You said in the last days that perilous times will come. "I will bless the Lord at all times" as it says in Psalms 34:1. You will resolve us, Father; this I know you will do in your time. Amen!

Let Love Reign available now through Author House!
Also look for *Let Love Reign Again.* Coming soon!

Demond M. James is the leader and visionary of Exousia of Christ International Kingdom Ministries, located in Chicago, Illinois, a fast-growing, fresh new ministry focused on building the Kingdom of God with the authority that Christ gave to the church with truth and love. He began his spiritual journey under the tutelage of Bishop Larry D. Trotter at Sweet Holy Spirit Church, where he serves as minister. He served as the youth pastor of 8th Day Eternal Glory Church on the south side of Chicago. His humble beginnings included being raised in a single-family home on the south side of Chicago in the inner city projects of Ida B. Wells and Robert Taylor Homes. He accepted the Lord at the young age of seven, was disconnected, and then reunited at the age of twenty-five. He studied music at Roosevelt University and received his ministerial license and biblical studies degree at Trinity Bible Institute. His message focuses on the Parousia of Christ with truth and love.